The Book of Five Arts

Al Case

QUALITY PRESS

For complete information on Matrixing the Martial Arts,
go to: MonsterMartialArts.com

ISBN: 9781796218336

TABLE OF CONTENTS

Introduction

I began the martial arts in 1967.

From the beginning I attempted to 'solve' the martial arts. I believe I am the only person to ever view the martial arts in this manner.

I would look at both sides of the technique; I would see if the technique would work on both sides of the body, right and left; I would see if the technique would work on both sides of a punch, the inside of the punch and the outside of the punch.

I would organize techniques to see if they could be adapted to other targets, or whether they were limited.

I would organize techniques according to whether they were punch, escape, grab, kick, or whatever, and then examine the art to see what 'blank' areas had no applicable techniques.

Eventually I came up with this thing called Matrixing. Matrixing is the application of logic to the martial arts, but it can be applied to any subject.

Matrixing uses, as its primary tool (but not the only tool) a Truth Table from Boolean logic. This provides a simple method for examining various parts of the martial arts, be it stances or blocks or attacks or techniques or whatever, to ensure that one has found all the parts of the art, or, to be more correct, has found the 'blank spots,' where there are no techniques.

This process enabled me to be positive that any art was complete and pure, not tainted by other art, not warped or altered or corrupted in any manner.

I applied Matrixing to a variety of arts, virtually every art I came across.

In this book are four of the main arts I matrixed, and a fifth art, designed by myself, as a solution to the martial arts.

These five arts present a picture of the arts that show the martial arts to be one art.

The martial arts in this book are, courtesy of 50 years of diligent research and discovery, a wholistic and integral subject with no blank spots.

If one thinks there is a blank spot in his art, there is a confusion of arts. And the only way to get rid of this blank spot, to fix their art, is to study sufficient individual arts, in pure fashion, without the taint or warp of other arts. If one does this then one will be able to mix the martial arts without confusion, keeping them pure, and yet enabling all arts to fulfill and support all other arts.

My personal pledge to you, studying matrixing will enable you to 'fix' your art, even if you don't know that it is broken.

Please be aware that some of the material in this book, texts and images, have been printed before, but they have been organized and compiled here so as to present the whole martial arts as a matrixed and integrated whole.

Al Case

KARATE

The ultimate aim of Karate lies not in victory or defeat, but in the perfection of the character of its participants.

Gichin Funakoshi

A NOTE ABOUT KARATE

I began my study of the martial arts with Chinese Kenpo Karate. This was in 1967, and most people didn't even know what Karate was.

I studied hard and within a year became an instructor. I then wrote the training manual for the school.

Eventually I found the Kang Duk Won, as taught by Robert J. Babich, and I entered the True Art.

As the years passed I earned my black belt, Bob (Mr. Babich) retired, and I began to learn and sort through various martial arts.

I opened my own school and taught the Kang Duk Won... and I found certain discrepancies in the art.

I was not of a mystical bent, I had no oral tradition; I was a child of western culture and the empirical method.

I set about revising what I had found.

I combined Karate with my studies of Wing Chun, Tai Chi Chuan and Aikido, and came up with something called 'The 16 Step Self Defense' method.

It was based on defending oneself in four directions (up, down, left and right)

In the four directions (of

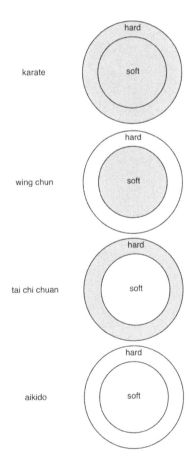

karate

wing chun

tai chi chuan

aikido

the compass), forward, backward, left and right.

And through four geometries of motion. These geometries of motion were based on four arts, Karate, Wing Chun, Tai Chi Chuan, and Aikido. The diagram in this chapter represents those motions. The whole system is presented in my book/video course titled 'Create Your Own Art.'

The system actually worked incredibly well, it was based on the accumulation of knowledge, not on arbitrary standards of 'quality.'

One very talented fellow went through the whole system (it was arranged in a check list fashion) in one week. Later on he traveled to Southern California and walked into a classical Shotokan school. He did some freestyle with some students, then with the head of the school, and was awarded his 3rd degree black belt. Shortly thereafter he became one of the instructors of the school.

So why did I put that system aside? Because people treated it like a whim, and I wanted to create die hard martial artists, not fellows and gals who did it for a quick fad.

One of the results of this period of my life was that I created Matrix Karate. This style of karate gave me what I wanted, die hard artists, and an art that was perfect and worked to a fare thee well.

In this book I have presented you with the heart and guts of the Matrix Karate system. These are the House Forms, and the accompanying theory as to how and why they are perfect examples of pure Karate.

THE SECRET OF KARATE

There is a center to your frame
push energy out and breath to grow flame

There is a circle in front of your frame
push out from your center and attacks you will tame

There are eight ways to set your strong arms
no one can enter without encountering harm

master these blocks to protect your body
it's all in your will not to be shoddy

The following diagram describes how the arms present a circle of blocks to protect the body. The arms should be aligned from punch, through arm, down the body, through the legs, and into the ground.

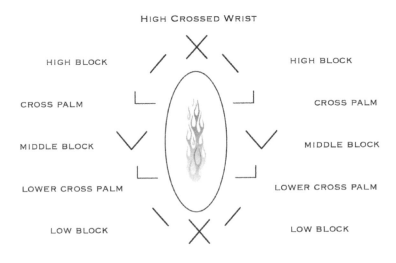

THE THEORY OF KARATE

First you must learn to sink to the earth
holding your ground determines your worth

then you bring energy into the center
breath with your motion let energy enter

keep the belly taut channel energy out
focus in your fists and never feel doubt

three types of power thrust drop and turn
put them together and intention you'll learn

strike with whole body not just the fist
the limbs are the fingers the trunk is a wrist

practice your moves to the finest detail
learning this way you'll never fail

THE HISTORY OF THE HOUSES

I created House One out of frustration with the current beginning forms.

Doing the kebons, or taikyokus, for months seemed too much.

The basics are easy.

I examined the basic forms of different systems and arts.

I spent much time examining Short One from Kenpo.

Short One wasn't bad, but the change of directions was confusing to the new student, and the blocks weren't always done right.

I had learned a system called Tan Toi (springy legs) from Northern Shaolin Kung Fu. These forms were all done on a line, and this simplicity made even complex moves easier to remember.

So I put the three basic blocks on a line and there it was: a perfect basic form. It could be done endlessly, gave me options to work on basic-basics, was easy to remember, and was instantly usable.

I then extrapolated further forms from that simple concept.

The real joy of this form was that it gave me an instant two man form. Students could work on the potentials of self defense right from the get go, and they would have instant feedback as to what was effective and what didn't work.

HOUSE ONE

To start this new art stand still in the room
aware of all corners to the universe you bloom

step to the rear and shoot the arm down
any you strike will wear a full frown

then shift to attack with weight, hip and thrust
whatever you hit is gonna bust

now bring up the foot and hold the pole hands
lower is inverted for the next in your plan

continue the step and shoot the block out
fist to override with a spirit shout

shift to the front driving the spike
into the attacker with all of your might

in the pole position the lower is a cup
to scoop a kick and lift a man up

drive up the arm and create a strong line
he'll hurt himself and you will feel fine

again do the strike the whole body hits
it'll shake his whole frame and shatter his wits

the hourglass stance with the buddha palm
do the form back a 1000 times strong

What you have been taught by listening to others' words
you will forget very quickly;
what you have learned with your whole body
you will remember for the rest of your life.

Gichin Funakoshi

2 MAN HOUSE ONE

Attacker steps forward with the left foot into a front stance and punches to the belly with the right hand.

Defender steps back with the right foot into a back stance and executes a left low block.

Attacker shifts/steps forward into a front stance and executes a right punch to the chest.

Attacker steps forward with the right foot into a front stance and punches to the chest with the left hand.

Defender steps back with the right foot into a back stance as he executes a right outward middle block.

Defender shifts/steps forward with the right foot into a front stance and executes a left punch to the chest.

Attacker steps forward with the left foot into a front stance as he executes a right punch to the face.

Defender steps back with the right foot into a back stance as he executes a left high block.

Defender shifts/steps forward with the left foot into a front stance and executes a right punch to the chest.

Defender becomes the attacker and steps forward with the left foot and strikes to the belly with the right hand.

Attacker becomes defender and steps back with the right foot into a back stance as he executes a left downward block.

The partners do the form in the opposite direction with roles reversed.

Do the form on both sides.

The form can be done with focus, with slight impact, as a 'plant and push' drill, and so on.

When the partners have the form down they can add a second punch in each position and utilize the buddha palm block (guard the face) prior to each regular strike.

Having students drill this form endlessly will replace the basic forms, such as kebons or taikyoku, and result in much more certainty and effectiveness of the basic blocks.

Drilling this form will prepare the students for freestyle quite rapidly.

TWO MAN HOUSE ONE IN PLACE

First you practice
one block at a time
stepping back and forth
in a straight line

Then you practice blocks
one, two, three
stepping together
and together you be

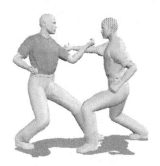

finally you will get
so good you don't walk
just simply stand
and let your fists talk

Striking in turn
you shift back and forth
stepping at the end

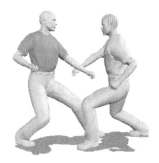

for all of your worth
you go low
then he goes out
you go high

then turn it about
strike without thought
of loss or defeat
train this way
and you can't be beat

HOUSE TWO

time to guard the bottom and top
crossing the wrists will swords and kicks stop

crossing hands low will catch a swift kick
grab heel and toe and throw with a twist

protect the head shift back with a block
loose-tight is the method to give his
bones shock

now it is time to return the force
push with the legs explode from the source

charge with the wrists catch arm not the blade
pull wrist and push elbow disarm and invade

Circle the hands as you draw back
strike knuckle to biceps and block his attack

punch the sternum bend it all in
hit what is soft not bone in the chin

bring up the foot and scoop up the hands
time to split push and kick in his glands

Down you grab snapping the fists
practice your snapping and you will crush
wrists

breath out with focus and lock snap the
kick if you want power tip and turn hip

the secret of power is to flick the fist
as if shaking water with just a little twist

turn into an elbow with a power stance
too close to fist an elbow is your chance

Now if you're smart and have entered in
split top from bottom and topple down him

Circle the arms to the Buddha Palm
Do the form back to a spiritual balm

Only through training will a person learn his own weaknesses...
He who is aware of his weaknesses will remain master of himself in
any situation.

Gichin Funakoshi

TWO MAN HOUSE TWO

He moves forward
to give you a punch
cross your wrists down
into his lunge

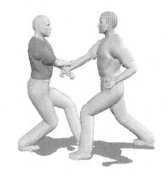

he'll throw a second strike
with a lead hand
you'll have to block quick
to keep your stand

then you will punch
but he is your friend
your fist on your chest
you'll push to just send

he'll take a big step
to strike down on your dome
again cross the wrists
protect your head bone.

follow quick with the left
he'll have to block out
strike on the biceps
or on his big snout

Now give it back
hard and fast
touch him soft
so he will last

Again he steps in
now pushing the chest
Step back with timing
and split his best

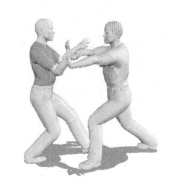

He's foiled but not done
he throws a lead hand.
blocking is fun
with a kick to the gland

he's hurt but keeps trying
with punch to the face
a high block applying
a punch wins the race

HOUSE THREE

first you should start with fists
that grow tight
as you progress learn to be light

slow and smooth drop the hand
down
all in the body energy goes down

connect to planet with block, hit
and kick
don't hit with a body part hit with
the planet

balance you'll have if you move
nice and
slow energy you'll have in
suspended flow

a strike with a block all
simultaneous
smaller units of time are
advantageous

now to step up and prepare the
hand
shoot from the center learn to
expand

bring the hand in it's called 'hidden
fist'
follow the body line too fast to
resist

the secret of power is sand in a
pipe
swirl and jerk all sand to the strike

four different blocks will grow
your potential
high, low, in, out combine the
essential

open the hands and learn to slap
grab
do it side to side don't move like a
crab

now drive down a pubic punch
his legs will collapse down he will
scrunch

circle the hands return to the
stance
do the form back in dedicated
dance

TWO MAN HOUSE THREE

If he attacks
and punches low
match his stance
and shoot your arm low

Then when he strikes
that is all right
block him across
and kick the bulbs light

now he throws high
with a punch for the head
simultaneous block
and strike him instead

one more step
and a punch to the middle
block and set up
 play him like a fiddle

Your block is hard
your fist is hidden
soon he will wish
an attack he didn't

Now twist and give him
the famous power punch
you can give him a turn
if he doesn't lose his lunch

Now step back
and let him come in
a universal block
will set up the win

grab his next punch
and twist with a hammer
break all his ribs
with a power horse slammer

he punches high
block and punch low
hit the pubic hard
and down he'll go

To search for the old is to understand the new.
Gichin Funakoshi

HOUSE FOUR

karate they say is all empty hands
but distance changes and so do plans

using an elbow is a short strike
up, down or side slash, smash or spike

entering in from either side
split top and bottom throw body and pride

if you are jammed and must get away
step quick and spin to start a new play

or you could slide and quick enter in
slipping the strike and striking the groin

stand like a mountain and growl like thunder
strike like lightening you'll split him asunder

in and out changing his mind
he won't find the distance but yours you will
find

strike with an elbow or use it to block
the trick is be brave and in walk

to stand and face and keep open eyes
that is an art as big as the skies

Now slash down and bring it around
make up your mind and he will fall down

now to balance your art on both sides
go the other way in never ending
strides

In battle, do not think that you have to win.
Think rather that you do not have to lose.

Gichin Funakoshi

THE MATRIX OF BLOCKS

You have seen the forms I created using Matrixing, now it is time to show you the actual matrix used in Matrix Karate. This specific matrix is called 'The Matrix of Blocks.'

	1	2
1	1 - 1	1 - 2
2	2 - 1	2 - 2

This is a matrix; it is actually called a Truth Table and it is found in Boolean Algebra. Boolean Algebra, incidentally, is used to describe three dimensional figures using only two dimensions.

Draw a cube on a piece of paper and you will understand this concept.

Or, just consider how the flat screen of a computer, or TV, can be used to show three dimensional objects and actions.

To use this Matrix in Karate I simply substitute blocks for numbers.

	Low	High
Low	L - L	L - H
High	H - L	H - H

By doing the these four blocks one understands the blocks, and every combination of them.

When I do them I have the attacker step forwards and strike with one hand, then the other. I step back and do one block on one side, then, when the second strike is thrown, I do a triangle step and block with the other side, then execute a punch with the non-blocking hand.

To the right is an example of 1-1, or low-low.

Now make a matrix using the four basic Karate Blocks: low, high, outward middle, inward middle.

You now have 16 blocks. Do them with the triangle step method I have just described, and you will understand, thoroughly, these basics.

Arts that are not-matrixed don't have this, they do a simple block until they know it, then they sort of cartwheel through various combinations with no regard for logic.

But if you use logic the blocks will be understandable ten times faster, and you will learn them, and know the martial arts, ten times faster.

And, yes, you can substitute different attacks, do kicks instead of punches, or elbows, or whatever.

Here is the matrix for the four blocks.

	low	high	outward	inward
low	low-low	low-high	low-out	low-in
high	high-low	high-high	high-out	high-in
outward	out-low	out-high	out-out	out-in
inward	in-low	in-high	in-out	in-in

Make a list and take turns going through the list with your partner.

I actually do four matrixes in Matrix karate. The second four blocks are X-low, X-high, palm, inverted forearm. Thus, the four matrixes are:

The first four blocks to the first four blocks (as above).
The first four blocks to the second four blocks.
The second four blocks to the first four blocks.
The second four blocks to the second four blocks.

Teaching them in these 'mini-matrixes works well. When the student is able to do the last matrix you can just tell him to do the complete matrix:

Eight blocks along the top to eight blocks down the left side.

You can create matrixes for techniques, moves from forms, even different arts, and arts to arts. Martrixing REALLY opens the door to the martial arts.

RHYTHMIC FREESTYLE

Freestyle is the actual fighting one learns when doing the martial arts.

One should practice the forms to learn the basic theory.

One should attempt to use that perfect theory presented by the forms in the various drills and techniques.

One should then adapt the perfection of concept into the chaos of real fighting, which should be closely approximated by freestyle.

There are many freestyle drills that help a student make this transition, help him apply martial arts concepts to actual self defense.

I prefer a specific method.

Karate ~ Rhythmic freestyle to freestyle.
Shaolin ~ Sticky Hands
Pa Kua Chang ~ man in center 'flowstyle.'
Tai Chi Chuan ~ Push Hands.
Monkey Boxing ~ Lop Sau.

I do, however, occasionally mix and match, according to the student's abilities and needs.

I don't however, mix arts. Students should learn the concepts of an art to the point where they understand it as a slice of the whole. When they learn sufficient slices they will be able to, without extra guidance, use the pieces appropriately.

When doing Rhythmic Freestyle the students take turns blocking and striking. this is NOT done at full speed, but rather half speed, or slower. The intent is not to fight, but to learn in a setting without pressure.

A second drill would be called 'Two Strike.' In Two Strike the partners will strike twice in succession before blocking twice in succession.

A third drill is called 'One Way.' In One Way one student attacks, slowly moving forward, while the other student blocks, slowly moving backward.

The fourth drill would be actual freestyle.

If this method is done correctly a student can learn to freestyle, quite adequately, within a few hours.

I originally designed freestyle this way because the original method, which was used in my instruction, was the teacher would beat the hell out of the student until the student finally figured something out. It would take months of losing, losing, losing.

With the Rhythmic freestyle method the students take turns winning, and the 'Joy of Combat' is eschewed for true learning.

SHAOLIN BUTTERFLY

Having conceived of his purpose,
a man should mentally mark out
a straight pathway to its achievement,
looking neither to the right nor the left.

James Allen

A NOTE ABOUT SHAOLIN

I had some 25 years of martial experience and was running my own school. One day a fellow walked in with 35 years experience. We quickly decided to trade arts.

My expertise was in Karate, with a LOT of assorted and unrefined other arts.

His expertise was in Shaolin and Tai Chi Chuan.

Some time later I would do with the Shaolin that he taught me (Fut Ga) what I had done with Karate: I would matrix it.

The result was the Shaolin Butterfly.

The Shaolin Butterfly was a matrix of footwork; exploring what would happen as I used the circular blocking methods of Shaolin in different directions.

It presents six different concepts extant in Shaolin, and does so by matrixing them with the central blocking motion of Shaolin, a circular (buzz saw) motion of a palm slap followed by a palm bone block.

The diagram you see in this chapter is an upgrade on the diagram I presented in the chapter on Karate, showing how I was developing in my understanding of how the progression of hard to soft actually worked.

Incidentally, the student is expected to figure out the two man forms for the Mantis and Choy & Li forms.

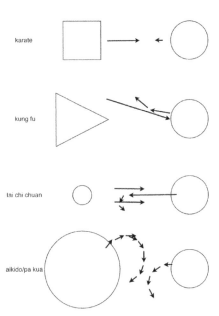

karate

kung fu

tai chi chuan

aikido/pa kua

THE BUTTERFLY FORM

There are six steps in the butterfly form
do them forever and you will transform

First like a monkey you run away
if he follows he'll rue the day

now you're gonna dodge by crossing the legs
just like a dragon walking on pegs

Now step around like a tiger charge
small angles that work and make a man large

Now step back out of the fray
the monkey decides to just go away

The arms travel to the Buddha Palm Block
it's hard to hit you when you sideways walk

Evading the punch with a possible spin
you're setting yourself up to charge on in

animals three and directions sly
a basic form you must apply

TWO MAN BUTTERFLY FORM

One steps forward and punches
with zest
the other sets back as easy as
rest

One steps in front and off to the
side
the other steps behind he's along
for the ride

Monkey then dragon then charge
like a tiger
changing hands as you go don't
ever stagger

do it for long learn about distance
the one who controls needs no
assistance

block on the wrist or stop the
biceps
or maybe the collar in time with the
steps

Almost done
but the end is the begin
so do it again
and again and again

THE FLOWER FORM

Standing at ready with no trace of sweat
you're about to give instead of get

one leg will go back and behind
a slight angulation works out just fine

Circle the hands and downward place
handle a kick by assuming a brace

now you charge into the hands
buzzsawing you go ripping his plans

poling the hands with small, subtle shifts
he'll miss without knowing your sideways drifts

slapping and blocking you slip centerline
over his hands you circle and climb

Now you are close and he wants to run
learn to confront and have some great fun

Circle the palm and take the last stride
he's gonna go for a quick fist ride

make a quick spear and learn to insert
the armpit becomes a world filled with hurt

Now it's time to get out of here
cover as you walk quick to the rear

if he still tries to follow you
you can still show him a thing or two

circle the arms while spinning in place
it's time to protect by downward brace

Now it is time to charge once again
a man confronts is a man who will win

spinning those hands run into the foe
just be aware as you inward go

be aware of his shoulders and enter them quick
to break a collarbone is like breaking a stick

train this way train with a thought
that always you'll win and never be caught

Now it is time to penetrate quick
his body is a melon your fingers are a stick

into him go aligning your bones
your fingers are like little, hard stones

Now it is time to get out of there
he wants to fight but you are nowhere

guarding you are set to turn in your place
and start all again the flowery pace

So spin and just do it again and again
this is the way to learn to win

able to block in any circumstance
by practicing just this sweet, simple dance

TWO MAN FLOWER FORM

Attacker kicks with the left leg.
Defender steps back with right leg
into leaning front stance as he
executes double palm block to shin.

Attacker brings leg back as he
punches with the right hand.
Defender moves forward as he
slaps the punch with his left palm.

The attacker completes stepping
back with the left foot as he
punches with the left hand.
The defender completes stepping
forward with the right leg as he
executes a butterfly palm block to
the attacker's wrist.

The attacker steps back as he
punches with the right hand.
The defender steps forward as he
executes a right smother block
and a left punch.

Attacker steps to the right with
his left foot.
Defender steps to the right with
his left foot.

Attacker takes a second step with
the right foot.
Defender spins in place.

Attacker turns and prepares to
execute a right kick.
Defender prepares the crossed
double palm down block.

Attacker kicks with the right leg.
Defender executes crossed
double palm down block.

Repeat the first part of the form
on the opposite side.

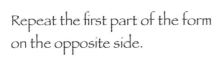

MANTIS FORM

Always be ready yet calm in the heart
this is the only way to start

Step to the side like in this book
instead of butterfly let your hand hook

Punch to the front as you step to the side
simultaneous palm as the feet go wide

do a butterfly hook on the other side
the outcome will be what you decide

Now step forward in a tiger crane stance
block to the rear to stop his advance

Retract the foot and turn to defend
if he attacks it'll be his end

Now pull back and sink in the horse
quick block and punch together of course

Shift as you step be quick with your hands
missing he won't know where he lands

Now take another tiger crane move
practice every day you'll always improve

Pull the foot back and spin around
back to begin another fine round

And don't forget when you've learned the form slick
to take it apart to find combat tricks.

Step back and to the side
into your hook he will glide.

He will advance with another
punch
Take a good horse and strike with
a crunch

Match his step with another match
his punch by the book

Step and disengage
let him get over his rage

Take a step and prepare for the
worst
He'll step two but he won't be first.

He comes around quick with a kick
Spin in place with a low block
trick.

He steps. forward and punches in
all over again from the begin

CHOY & LI

Always be willing to face your man square
yet able to get out of there

Step to the side with an inverted low
if he kicks away he'll go

Bring in the rear and twist to the front
that'll stop an attacker's stunt

Shift to the front roll the right hand
slapping it down like a quick moving fan

Taking a step you slap with the left
moving with speed your touch is quite deft

Now step back and punch in a horse
sinking is how you increase your force

Step with the left and invert the low
across the butterfly pattern you go

Now take another step as you swing
the arms in circles to block and fling

With the front foot step to the fore
practice both sides to be good at war

Swinging the hands your hands really roll
upward one way then downward you go

this is the secret of Choy and of Li
of fighting to win without all the glee

just practice until it is easy as pie
windmilling the arms till spirit fills sky

This is the way the monks of old
did practice until the spirit turned gold

Pay attention now to what I have said
do the form again until light is your tread.

Do this form 'two man style,' as you did with the other
three forms, with a partner 'feeding' you strikes as you move
through the form.

LOP SAU AND STICKY HANDS

Lop Sau means 'rolling fists.' I have seen bits and pieces of this drill, truncated versions and alterations, in all manner of arts. Specifically, but not exclusively, Wing Chun and Jeet Kune Do.

Through Matrixing I was able to create the complete drill.

It is okay to skip ahead to the Monkey Boxing section and learn the drill for practice with the Butterfly art.

I originally taught Sticky Hands, from Wing Chun Kung Fu, with the Butterfly.

I replaced it with Lop Sau for the simple reason that Lop Sau is ten times easier to learn, and ten times more combat realistic.

When a student has Lop Sau down I frequently go into Sticky Hands.

TEACUP PA KUA CHANG

Mind is the Master power that moulds and makes,
And Man is Mind, and evermore he takes
The tool of Thought, and, shaping what he wills,
Brings forth a thousand joys, a thousand ills:--
He thinks in secret, and it comes to pass:
Environment is but his looking-glass.

James Allen

A NOTE ABOUT PA KUA CHANG

I began my studies of Pa Kua Chang with a book. I had become fascinated with descriptions of the art in magazines, and was determined, though there were no teachers about, to learn the art.

I progressed through videos, observed (without being observed) various individuals, and walked the circle for hours a day for years.

One day a fellow walked into my school and said he knew Pa Kua, that he studied a certain style and had done so for years.

After a short but friendly talk we agreed to compare styles.

He went through his movements, liquid and powerful, then I went through mine.

He complimented me and asked where I had studied. His jaw dropped when he discovered I was self-taught.

When I asked him for any pointers he merely said, 'I can't teach you anything, you already know it.'

When I finally decided to write a book (and do a video) on my Pa Kua, I included three parts, one on basics, one on a concept of motion I had developed, and one on the

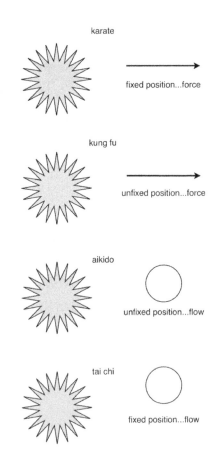

karate — fixed position...force

kung fu — unfixed position...force

aikido — unfixed position...flow

tai chi — fixed position...flow

classical Eight Animals.

In this book I give you the concept I developed which I refer to as Teacup Pa Kua. I think you will find that learning concepts is superior to learning techniques.

In this chapter the diagram shows how I had discovered that each art had specific concepts of motion and geometry.

introduction

One of the things most wrong with the Wudan style arts is that they are out gradient.

By this, I mean that they are so advanced, and yet they have not offered proper instruction in basics.

Karate has basics, and these basics can be broken down into basic-basics.

Pa Kua, however, is less well grounded in basics. And, as time goes on, this matter of basics becomes less and less important...and so it becomes ever harder to ground the art, and to even hope to find basic-basics.

That being said, there are three styles of Pa Kua that I teach, but I focus on the 'Teacup' method I show you here.

One, the Ten Hands method, is designed to establish basic matrixing theory. Further, the intent is to set the student up so that the arms become unbendable, and that energy flows through the ten perfect arm configurations.

Two, the Teacup method, is designed to further develop matrixing theory, and to refine the creation and flow of energy, and to set up basic self-defense modes.

Third, the Eight Animals method, is classical, but refined through the first two methods I teach, and further development of matrixing, and to more fully explore the self-defense content.

CHAPTER ONE

The basic matrix of Teacup Pa Kua is based on three arm positions.

Hooked Low is 1.
Middle Palm Up is 2.
High is 3.

Thus, the Matrix looks like this:

low/low	middle/low	high/low
low/middle	middle/middle	high/middle
low/high	middle/high	high/high

These are the nine positions of Teacup Pa Kua. They will give a different feel and build of energy, and yet they are obviously usable as simple block and strike self-defense, and they can obviously be developed into more complex defensive techniques.

Though there are nine positions listed, it should be noted that one of the positions (high/low) is awkward and doesn't translate well. Thus, you will see only eight teacup movements in this art.

THE FIRST CUP

Stand on the circle in a natural stance.

Raise the hands and hold them as if holding saucers and teacups.

Turn the left foot towards the next spot on the circle and pivot the body slightly to the left.

Step to the next spot on the circle with the right foot. The arms should be gradually spreading wider apart.

Pivot to the left, spreading the hands wider, synchronizing the body parts so they move together

Pivot to a back stance facing to the left, the hands should be spread so that they are unbendable, and there is an unbendable curve around the shoulders, also.

Pivot back to the right, through an hourglass stance. Keep the arms spread. Extend energy through your arms forever.

Continue the pivot through a back stance to the right

Pivot the right foot towards the next spot on the circle as you shift the weight onto the right foot. The arms should start coming together gradually.

Step to the next spot on the circle with the left foot. The arms will close, the right towards the center of the circle and the left augmenting at the elbow. Keep the palms up, (now and always) as if you are holding saucers and teacups.

CHAPTER TWO

When you bring the cup around and swing the left leg out and around to take the next step on the circle, there should be a 'floating' sensation. This is similar to the Karate 'sand in the pipe' concept, but done Pa Kua style.

Imagine a pipe half filled with sand, hold the pipe upright and move it so that all the sand hits one side of the pipe at the same time. There is more data on this on the Matrix Karate course, and the material in the Karate course should prepare you for this concept. Karate is the proper gradient for learning this easily and efficiently.

At any rate, the idea is to have your body half filled with 'sand' (energy), and to 'swirl' it, and to learn how build it in movements and to use it in techniques.

THE SECOND CUP

Walk the circle until you are one step
beyond the base of the circle.

Pivot to the left, spreading the hands wider,
synchronizing the body parts so they move
together.

Pivot to a back stance facing to the left, the
left hand rotates upward into a high block,
the right hand is in the middle position.

Pivot back to the right, the left hand swings
out and around so that both hands are in the
spread middle position.

Continue the pivot through a back stance
to the right.

Pivot the right foot towards the next spot
on the circle as you shift the weight onto
the right foot. The arms should start coming
together gradually.

Step to the next spot on the circle with the
left foot. The arms will close, the right
towards the center of the circle and the left
augmenting at the elbow. Keep the palms up, (now
and always) as if you are holding saucers and
teacups.

CHAPTER THREE

To make this art work one must use the body as one unit (CBM--Coordinated Body Motion--again, see Matrix Karate)

On some moves you can simply keep the hand above the foot, and move them as one.

Some moves, however, are going to entail starting the body parts at the same time, moving them at slightly different rates of speed, then stopping them at the same time.

At any rate, if you turn the body in one direction, the hands should move in a likewise manner.

A note: there are two directions you can twine for either hand. Go ahead and explore the different twining and combinations of twinings. The rule that should ultimately define what you are doing, however, is to move the hands in the same direction as the body. This will increase Coordinated Body Motion...and Intention.

THE THIRD CUP

Walk the circle until you are one step
beyond the base of the circle.

Pivot to the left, spreading the hands wider,
synchronizing the body parts so they move
together

Pivot to a back stance facing to the left, the
left hand pivots down to parry, the right hand
is in the middle position.

Pivot to the right as you continue the circle
of the left arm to a high position. The left
arm arm is in the extended middle position.

Pivot the right foot towards the next spot
on the circle as you shift the weight onto
the right foot. The left arm continues its
motion
until your arms are in the middle spread position.

Step to the next spot on the circle with the
left foot. The arms will close, the right towards
the center of the circle and the left augmenting at the
elbow. Keep the palms up, (now and always) as if
you are holding saucers and teacups.

CHAPTER FOUR

Circling the body, spiraling the arms, all in the same direction, makes the body move as one unit and builds intention.

As you achieve this you chip away at the real core of Pa Kua...building a separate universe.

It is easy to isolate your own universe this way. Just be integral, learn how not to have any counter motion in your own frame, and you will learn how not to have any counter motion in your thoughts.

This is not to say that you can't build a universe out of contrary motions, but it won't make as much sense, and it won't lead you onward on the correct Martial Path.

(If you wish to learn how to isolate body parts in contrary motions and still use them to build intention you should study Karate.)

Just a short spat of Pa Kua and you feel the motion, and you can give yourself up to the motion. The more you give yourself up to this purity of motion the more you build your own separate universe.

Just a note, one use of this separate universe is when somebody bear hugs you, and you walk as you will, flinging him off as you desire. Have somebody grab you (lightly in the beginning) and practice this. You will shortly see what I mean.

THE FOURTH CUP

Walk the circle until you are one step
beyond the base of the circle.

Pivot to the left, spreading the hands wider,
synchronizing the body parts so they move
together

Pivot to a back stance facing to the left, both
hands parry.

Pivot back to the right, the left hand swings
out and around to a high block the left hand
swings to the middle position.

Pivot the right foot towards the next spot on the circle as you shift the weight onto the right foot. The left arm should continue its circling until you are in the middle spread arms position.

Step to the next spot on the circle with the left foot. The arms will close, the right towards the center of the circle and the left augmenting at the elbow. Keep the palms up, (now and always) as if you are holding saucers and teacups.

CHAPTER FIVE

To create a two pole universe, one which is separate from the 'real' universe, you should have a partner. You circle one another and watch each others eyes. You will shortly become aware of the world behind your partner sliding. Let it slide, concentrate on your partner, and build the new reality between you.

THE FIFTH CUP

Walk the circle until you are one step beyond the base of the circle.

Pivot to the left, spreading the hands wider, synchronizing the body parts so they move together

Pivot to a back stance facing to the left, both hands execute high blocks.

As you pivot to the right into an hourglass stance swing the left arm out and around to the middle position and the left arm in and through to a parry position.

As you continue pivoting into a back stance, the left hand continues its motion through a parry to a high block the left hand swings to the middle position.

Pivot the right foot towards the next spot on the circle as you shift the weight onto the right foot. The left arm should continue its circling until you are in the middle spread arms position.

Step to the next spot on the circle with the left foot. The arms will close, the right towards the center of the circle and the left augmenting at the elbow. Keep the palms up, (now and always) as if you are holding saucers and teacups.

CHAPTER SIX

One thing you will notice is that the body becomes a motor.

A motor is defined by two poles, between which there is tension (pull or push).

As you walk the circle, and make the transition from pole to pole, you will feel energy twine up the leg, then twine down the other leg. You must make sure you move synchronously, so that the energy will translate to the arms correctly.

THE SIXTH CUP

Walk the circle until you are one step
beyond the base of the circle.

Pivot to the left, spreading the hands wider,
synchronizing the body parts so they move
together

Pivot to a back stance facing to the left, the
left hand is in the middle position, the right hand
twines to the high block position.

Pivot to the right into a back stance, the left
hand continues its motion through a parry to
a high block the left hand swings through a
parry to the middle position.

Pivot the right foot towards the next spot
on the circle as you shift the weight onto
the right foot. The left arm should
continue its circling until you are in the middle
spread arms position.

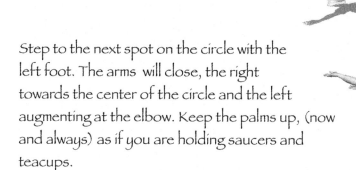

Step to the next spot on the circle with the
left foot. The arms will close, the right
towards the center of the circle and the left
augmenting at the elbow. Keep the palms up, (now
and always) as if you are holding saucers and
teacups.

CHAPTER SEVEN

The movements in this book, as defined by pictures, gives the idea that you are moving from position to position.

Really, you are moving THROUGH position after position.

You are liquid, rolling through the motions.

This causes the muscle to undergo extended suspension of weight, which is better for the muscle than virtually any other kind of weight lifting.

The key here, however, not that you are lifting weight, but that you are channeling awareness through the body.

Channel awareness, and energy starts to follow, and then you have some serious Art.

THE SEVENTH CUP

Walk the circle until you are one step
 beyond the base of the circle.

Pivot to the left, spreading the hands wider,
synchronizing the body parts so they move
together

Pivot to a back stance facing to the left, the
left hand is in the middle position, the right
 hand hooks over to a parry.

As you pivot to the right into an hourglass
stance the left arm hooks over into a parry,
and the right rotates up to a middle position.

Continue pivoting into a back stance, the left
hand continues its motion through a parry to
a high block the left hand stays in the middle
position.

Pivot the right foot towards the next spot
on the circle as you shift the weight onto
the right foot. The left arm should continue its
circling until you are in the middle spread arms
position.

Step to the next spot on the circle with the
left foot. The arms will close, the right
towards the center of the circle and the left
augmenting at the elbow. Keep the palms up,
(now and always) as if you are holding
saucers
and teacups.

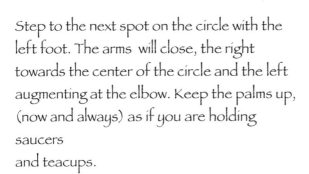

CHAPTER EIGHT

You may have noticed that when walking with the arms positioned as if holding a large pot, you began to generate tremendous heat.

In Teacup Pa Kua you can create this same type of heat in the palm of your hand if you concentrate on the palm that is inside the circle.

You may experience other sensations, prickling, etc., and that is okay.

One thing you may want to do, to aid in this process, is to concentrate on pushing the weight up one leg, into the tan tien, and down the other leg. Make sure you move slow, and breath out as you create heat, in as you walk (keeping the hips thrust forward and the belly taut)

I call this 'Boiling the Tea,' and it is a great way to generate energy.

THE EIGHTH CUP

Walk the circle until you are one step beyond the base of the circle.

Pivot to the left, spreading the hands wider, synchronizing the body parts so they move together

Pivot to a back stance facing to the left, the left hand hooks to a parry, the right hand twines to a high block.

Pivot to the right into a back stance, the left hand continues its motion through a parry to a high block the right twines down to a parry.

Pivot the right foot towards the next spot
on the
circle as you shift the weight onto the right foot.
The arms should continue circling to the middle
spread arms position.

Step to the next spot on the circle with the
left foot. The arms will close, the right
towards the center of the circle and the left
augmenting at the elbow. Keep the palms up, (now
and always) as if you are holding saucers
and teacups.

MAN IN CENTER 'FLOWSTYLE'

Flowstyle is based multiple man freestyle in Aikido.

The techniques, however, are based on the techniques of Monkey Boxing and the circle walking of Pa Kua Chang.

Thus, there are no techniques where you lead an opponent unresisting to his demise; rather, there are techniques which call for the same flow and effortlessness, but they are based on more combat realistic techniques.

We do set up the same back rolls and front rolls and breakfalls out of the techniques so that the flow can go on without injury.

The drill can be begun with just two men. Then, when one has become familiar with the grabs, one can introduce multiple men into the exercise.

CONCLUSION

I teach three separate forms of Pa Kua.

Ten Hands Pa Kua introduces Matrixing, and teaches one how to create unbendable arms in stances.

Teacup Pa Kua more firmly establishes Matrixing, and teaches one more about CBM.

Eight Animals is the classical mode. It is, however, difficult to do unless one has done the work of Ten Hands and Teacup.

Teacup Pa Kua is part of the Butterfly Pa Kua Chang book/video course.

There is additional work, aligning Pa Kua with the art I developed called 'The Infinite Fist,' which is specific to 'Diagram Boxing,' which is on the Create Your Own Art Course.

The Create Your Own Art Course is an amazing piece of work.

A note concerning the Create Your Own Art Course: the picture quality of the videos is poor.

Technology was not up to the task back then.

You can still see the movements, but everything is fuzzy.

MATRIX TAI CHI CHUAN

Do nothing until nothing is undone

The Tao

A NOTE ABOUT TAI CHI CHUAN

There was a fellow in Japan, a high ranking black belt, who decided to go to China and study Tai Chi. His fellow karateka curled their lips in disgust.

Years later he returned to Japan and resumed teaching Karate. His fellow karatekas were heartened to see that he had finally come to his senses.

I always loved this story, one fellow going against the group and discovering the truth; one fellow caught in a Closed Combat System, but refusing to be blinded.

As for myself, I will tell you that even though I had studied many arts, matrixed many arts, I didn't really understand the arts until I had done Tai Chi Chuan.

I began about 1974, and I applied Tai Chi concepts to my other arts. I did Karate Tai Chi style, I did various meditations, I explored concepts religiously. And I will tell you, at this point, that Douglas Wile's book on Tai Chi Touchstones shows how simple physics can be made mystical. This is a valuable lesson, and can severely impact any art, if understood. And it can be understood through matrixing, and defining simple concepts of western physics.

In this book I show how to translate Tai Chi Chuan into simple, but effective, combat moves. Understood in this fashion and Tai Chi becomes a tremendously effective combat art.

And, people who study Tai Chi for health, without the combat applications, are robbing themselves. Without the intention of combat, the intention to run energy through the body is weak. Learn the combat applications and energy, including healthy and healing energy, will be ten times stronger than if one merely does the motions for 'health.'

The digram in this chapter illustrates how I was putting the concepts of the progression of hard to soft into a complete picture, a whole and connected art.

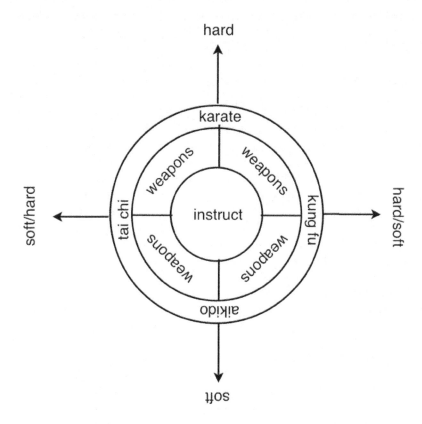

One might think the 'weapons should have been on the outside of the circle, and they would be correct, but I was still formulating weapons from within the separate arts.

MATRIX TAI CHI CHUAN

Andy is going to learn Tai chi. It will take him a week or so. He won't be polished, but he will understand what the moves mean, and how to use them. He will be, literally, years ahead of the poor student who still learns by the old 'monkey see monkey do' method.

RAISE HANDS
Sink the knees slightly, raise the hands to the front. Breath in as you raise the hands, breath out when you lower the hands. Get the feeling of standing waist deep in an ocean of Chi and feeling the rise and fall of the ocean of chi lift and lower your hands. Technically, you're supposed to do this three times. But, hey, do it until you feel good about it. Like, a few thousand times. Right?

LOWER HANDS
Step back with one foot as you lower the hands. The right foot, in this example. Make sure you breath out. Strive to keep balance on the front foot until you are ready to shift to the rear foot.

ROLL BACK
Circle the hands out and around
and bring them together as if
holding a guitar.

BRUSH KNEE
Circle the hands as you shift
forward into the brush knee
posture. This one you should push
forward, then turn the waist. But
here's the key...you MUST
achieve an unbendable
arm...FROM THE TAN TIEN!

If you do this you will instantly feel
a weight, or a surge, or a bubbling,
in the tan tien. The tan tien is the
energy generator for the body,
and this means that you have just
turned it on, made it work, and now you are making chi. If you
don't get this sensation then you aren't making chi.

WHITE SNAKE
Circle the rear hand in an oval to
the front, circle the front hand
outside and bring it inwards.
I know, everybody think the white
snake should have the front hand
moving outwards. But it doesn't
have to. But if you feel that you
must, then tweak your motions,
figure out how to move so that you get that thrusting outward
block type of thing. 'Sup to you.

FAIR LADY
Shift forward, figuring out when to
push and when to turn, keeping
the arms unbendable, and circle
the front hand to a high block,
and oval the rear hand to a palm
strike.

There is a pulsing feel to Tai Chi sometimes. you can make this
happen a lot, or smooth it out. Some people like to work on the
pure circle, I prefer giving a subtle circle or pulse at the end or
beginning of some techniques. Do these exercises until you have
choice as to whether to pulse or be still in motion.

POLE POSITION
Shift back, circling the right hand
out and around and down to cover
the groin, and lifting the rear hand
slightly to cover the face. You
should resemble a person holding
a pole.

HOLDING THE BALL
After you shift backwards to the
pole position, turn slightly and
assume the Holding the Ball
position. The top hand continues
to cover the face, the low hand
scoops slightly.
You should be feeling chi wash
back and forth inside your body
when you move back and forth.
Learn to relax and let the chi
happen.

WARD OFF
Shift forward, circling the hands
so that it is as if you are stroking
the tail of a bird perched on your
forearm. This is a very classic

move. It is also called Stroking the Horse's Mane, or changed
slightly into Slant Flying.
Remember, differentiate when you should push, when you should
turn, and always keep that flowing sensation in the unbendable
arm.

WHITE CRANE
Circle the arms so that the front
hand is in the low block position
and the rear hand is in the high
position.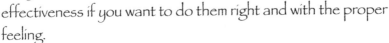
You have several options here,
and while you will practice
however you wish, you must
analyze the moves for
effectiveness if you want to do them right and with the proper
feeling.
You can shift back without turning the hips. Or you can shift back
and turn the hips. Depends on if you are blocking hard or soft.
You can also choose to circle in or out with the arms.
you will need that little circle within a circle shift to make these
things happen.

SINGLE WHIP
Shift forward, circling the arms
until the rear hand is in a whip, and
the front hand is in a palm thrust.

MONKEY KICK (scoop)
Shift back and circle the hands
until they scoop in front of the
body.

MONKEY KICK
Kicks are interesting things.
People like to fill the with energy,
but in Tai Chi you want to make
them light and flicking. When you
are on one foot you need good
weight sinking (grounding), and
good balance.

CROSS HANDS
Put the foot down and scoop the
hands over and down.

OPEN KICK
Bring the leg up and circle the
hands up and push outward all at
the same time. It is like you are on
a puffy weed, energy comes up,
and explodes form the center, all
limbs in equilibrium.

From the previous ten postures you can see that there are five 'lines' in Matrix Tai Chi Chuan.

Roll Back to Brush Knee
White Snake to Fair Lady
Pole Position to Ward Off
White Crane to Single Whip
Open Kick to Monkey Kick

Drill the student until they can do the lines blindfolded, then introduce them to the Nine Square. The Nine Square will teach them how to move in directions other than forward and back.

BASIC APPLICATIONS
HARD STYLE

SET POSITION
Andy is on the left, Ryan in
on the right. The set up
can be right foot forward
to right foot forward, or
right foot forward to left
foot forward. This is also known as cross side and same side, or
opening or closing, etc.
The point is that you should be able to make the techniques work
for as many potential 'sides' as there are.

ROLL BACK
All Andy does is use roll
back as a block. From this
point he can punch or kick
or whatever. Truth, this is
sort of bad karate, but it is
adequate for the moment.
As the student becomes
polished the block will
become more efficient than

a Karate block. For beginners, however...it provides good self
defense.

BRUSH KNEE

Here is the forward move, Brush Knee, done as a straight forward block and attack. The key here is that to learn simultaneous block and strike movements is actually an advanced thing. It requires

that you see the opponent's body a long time before the strike happens, that you have an intuitive feel for this sort of thing. This requires mushin no shin (mind of no mind), which is a real zen, 'in the moment' state of mind. Mushin no shin is much more easily attained through Matrix Karate than a study of Tai Chi. Thus, I tell people to do Karate first, then go into Tai Chi. You can make the transition from block and strike to simultaneous block and strike much easier this way.

Of course, if you already know Tai Chi, it is easy to go back and pick up the pieces, but most Tai Chi-ists seem to have an innate snobbery about them which precludes them doing this.

At any rate, the actual sequence of motion that should be followed when one does the various martial arts will go something like this:

Karate ~ block and strike
Wing Chun ~ simultaneous block and strike arms only
Tai Chi Chuan ~ simultaneous block and strike with the whole body.

The trick is to understand how your art works and be able to plug it in to this table. This is difficult because most arts art vast mixes of techniques, with random samplings of timing and distance and technique. This is why Matrixing is incredibly valuable; it separates arts into their individual concepts.

Even if you can't quite manage to separate your art (there's too many ranges and distances and so on), the effect of matrixing on the mind makes the student able to start blending what he does, and finding a hidden logic that is really himself.

WHITE SNAKE

A simple parry and a finger strike to the throat. Yes, you can make a fistic uppercut if you wish, but Tai Chi is based on delicacy. It is a knitting needle, not a bludgeon. You can also simply use the move as an inward middle block, but this is going a long way towards Karate.

FAIR LADY

This is a straight forward enter with a high block and a palm. The key is to enter far enough, and to commit your whole weight, plus whatever energy pulse you can generate with your body.

Learning how far to move in, or back, is key to successful Tai Chi Chuan.

POLE POSITION 1
You look like you are
holding a pole in pole
position, but these are
simple blocks.
In the above example Andy
is blocking a punch to the
face. From here he can roll
his hands and punch, or
work any number of block.

WARD OFF
Ward off feeds easily from
Pole Position. In this
example Andy is pushing
forward and striking to the
ribs (or kidney) with a
rounded arm that could be
translated into a chop.
I probably should have
presented this as a block

and chop, but Tai Chi is simultaneous, and block and chop, once
again, is karate.

WHITE CRANE
Here Ryan kicks, and
Andy uses White Crane to
block the kick. From here
Andy could easily come
down with a right back
wrist to the front of Andy's
face.

SINGLE WHIP
Hard to see, but Andy has
caught Ryan with the whip,
and is executing a palm
strike to his chest.

MONKEY KICK

A simple outward middle block and a quick snap kick. Better to the groin, but anyplace there is a body wanting to be hurt is fine.

OPEN KICK

Change the blocks slightly, and use the heel. You can also set this kick up as a reverse crescent (swinging the foot sideways).

For the Monkey Kick and the Open Kick we won't be showing soft applications when we get to that section. Yes, you could set

down behind a knee, or somehow trip somebody, but, really, a kick doesn't lend itself to many throws, and those would be very special and usually not useful.

NINE SQUARE DIAGRAM FOOTWORK

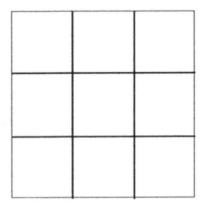

When you do the following moves, or techniques on the nine square, you want to let the circles flow one to another, no stops or reversals. Try to make everything flow from one posture to the next physically, and it will make it work in your chi projection.
I will tell you about chi projection after this section. Here is the nine square diagram.

Draw one on the ground. The squares should be shoulder width apart. You can make the squares shorter or larger as you become more practiced. Shorter for close in work, longer for deep stance, chi generating work.

Here are the beginning steps for nine square diagram footwork.

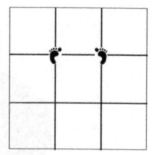

First Nine Square ~ Stand on the front of the middle square.

Second Nine Square ~ Step back with the right foot and execute a roll back, then a brush knee.

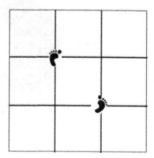

Third Nine Square ~ Turn the left foot in, then the right foot out as you pivot to the right, execute a roll back, then a brush knee.

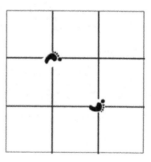

Fourth Nine Square ~ Step back with the right foot to the next square (right side middle).

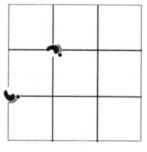

Continue the roll back/brush knee sequence going around the nine square diagram in a figure eight. (diagram on next page.)

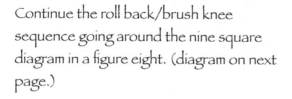

As I said, you are doing a figure eight on the nine square. This will include thirteen squares, starting on the center and finishing on the center.

Now, while I have you go backwards, you can obviously adapt this diagram. You can go forward, turn the eight on the side, start going diagonal, whatever you wish. The main thing is to explore the roll back/brush knee sequence. Build chi energy, reel silk, and sink into the movement until it becomes you.

And here's where the fun comes in.

Do this exercise for all 25 matrix combinations. Find the ones that give the most energy. Find the ones that work.

Thus, the student ends up with 25 mini forms that take these motions apart like they have never been taken apart before.

THE FOUR SQUARE DIAGRAM

You can pick any geometry you want to create your art on: square, triangle, circle...whatever.

I use a specific sequence of geometries.

Karate is square

Shaolin is triangular.

Pa Kua is circular.

Tai Chi is the nine square.

But I also use other shapes, or combinations of shapes.

At this point, move away from footwork and discuss the four square diagram and how it relates to Tai Chi...and thus to other arts.

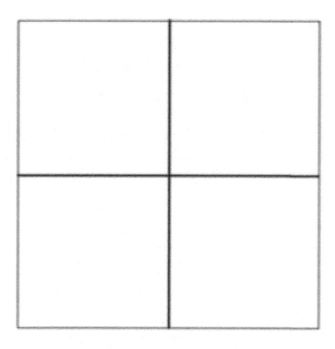

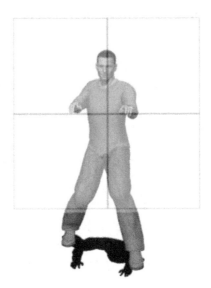

This divides the fighter into quadrants, and one arm defends (attacks) in each quadrant. It is a very good way to analyze the potentials of the human body.

This concept is utilized heavily in Wing Chun. It uses a four square for each arm, and there is a complete strategy for which arm protects which quadrant when.

Unfortunately, while Wing Chun is very thorough in its specific art, for the specific geometries of motion in the Wing Chun mode, it doesn't take into account all the potentials offered by Karate, Aikido, Tai Chi, and the various other arts.

So I took it and used it in Karate. And then in Shaolin and Tai Chi and whatever other art I happened to come across.

But I have to say that, while I had learned of the Boolean Algebra device known as a truth table in high school, it wasn't until I saw the four square offered in Wing Chun Kung Fu that the lights began going on.

I eventually expanded it to cover other arts, all potentials of motion, and matrixing was born.

And I began to impose various geometries on the body and on motion. For instance, here is the Nine Square imposed on the body.

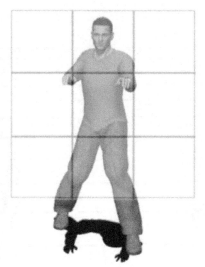

But I use the Nine Square more in Monkey Boxing than in Tai Chi. In Tai Chi I tend to use the four square, as imaged on the previous page.

On the following pages are a few examples.

Brush Knee

Fair Lady

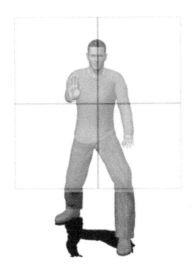
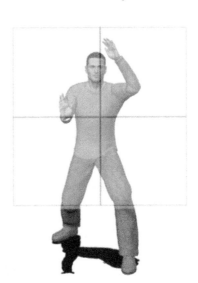

Obviously, you can figure out how each posture can fill the various squares of the Four Square Diagram.

fair lady	single whip
white crane brush knee	white snake pole position

Go ahead and place the remaining TCC postures in the four square diagram.

And, if you wish, you can expand on this concept with other diagrams. For instance:

Fair Lady	Pole Position	Single Whip
Roll Back		White Snake
Brush Knee	Pole Position	White Crane

Lots of points to be made here:

What do you do about blank squares that arise for specific ranges?

If the opponent was kicking, what defenses should you use?

If the opponent was hooking his punches, what defenses should you use?

If the opponent was using elbows, what defenses should you use?

And knives, and swords, and even guns...what defenses should you use?

Now go back over the earlier arts in this book, define them by using the four square, or the nine square, or other geometric patterns.

The only real problem with these diagrams, however, is that often the matrix isn't complete. To have a complete matrix one would have to have strikes to all four squares with the front hand while in the front stance.

And the back hand.

And out of the back stance.

And so on.

Tai Chi Chuan fits certain parameters, uses certain types of energy, and the boxes just aren't all filled.

But the art is complete enough that one may use it.

And the real solution to this problem is to study other arts (matrix other arts) so that you can use other arts to fill the boxes.

However, one doesn't EVER combine arts, try to make Shaolin into Tai Chi, or that sort of thing. If one does that the arts tend to mush, and we end up with the massive problems presented by the martial arts of today.

Arts don't work, arts are hard to teach and hard to learn, arts contest for which is better, confusion as to what art to use in what situation arises, and so on.

If you want to combine arts you don't. Instead, learn each art thoroughly, by itself, such as is presented in this book, and then keep the arts separate.

If you do this you will have no confusion, and each art will tend to pop up by itself, right time and right place, the appropriate strategy and geometry for whatever situation, when it is needed.

Understand it this way: each art has a type of motion and energy, and if you take a block with, say, the motion and energy of Tai Chi and try to put it in the matrix of Karate, the result is confusion. The concepts don't work; the principles oppose.

But if you make a matrix for each art, and understand each art thoroughly, you won't have to think, it will become intuitive. That is just the way the mind works when it is presented with the correct data in the correct order/fashion.

Let me sum it up this way.

I often talk about the 'blank spots' in a martial art, and now, upon examining the matrix of TCC techniques, either four square or nine square, you can see how I isolate the various blank spots.

After I find the blank spots I decide whether to create technique to fill them, or shift arts, or whatever.

And, one last word about this matrix of Tai Chi...to be totally and utterly honest, the Matrix of Karate is ten times better than the Matrix of Tai Chi for the hard strikes and blocks. You will understand this if you study Matrix Karate and compare it to Matrix Tai Chi.

Different arts with different matrixes, different blank spots, and different ways of filling them.

See, it's sort of ridiculous when somebody says one art is better than another. All arts have specific purposes, and only when one has sufficient matrixes in all the arts do they become one art and start to function as a single complete martial art.

HOW TO MATRIX THE BASICS OF TAI CHI CHUAN

The truth is that there are no advanced techniques, there are just better basics.

The only proviso to this is that arts like Tai Chi, 'internal arts,' as they are sometimes called, have different basics, basics that don't agree with harder arts.

For instance, the art of Tai Chi is an 'absorbing' art, the technique is drawn in to the body, as opposed to, say, karate, where the art is expended from the Tan Tien, pushed away from the body.

But it is not a matter of better basics, just different basics, basics that people reared in this 'force obsessed' universe don't always understand.

A real matrix is a truth table, and it combines potentials until there are no overlooked or misunderstood potentials. This gives a complete and thorough understanding of how basics work, thus validating the concept that there are no advanced techniques, just better basics.

On the following page is the Matrix for the basics.

Please remember that I teach the simple self defenses when a student is learning on lines and simple triangles.

When the student is adept at motion and simple self-defense moves I move the form onto the nine square, and do the Matrix of Blocks (for Tai Chi).

	brush knee	fair lady	ward off	single whip	open kick
roll back	roll back/ brush knee	roll back/ fair lady	roll back/ ward off	roll back/ single whip	roll back/ open kick
white snake	white snake/ brush knee	white snake/ fair lady	white snake/ ward off	white snake/ single whip	white snake/ open kick
pole position	pole position/ brush knee	pole position/ fair lady	pole position/ ward off	pole position/ single whip	pole position/ open kick
white crane	white crane/ brush knee	white crane/ fair lady	white crane/ ward off	white crane/ single whip	white crane/ open kick
monkey kick	roll back/ monkey kick	monkey kick/ fair lady	monkey kick/ ward off	monkey kick/ single whip	monkey kick/ open kick

I have put the attacks across the top, and the 'blocks' down the side. You can arrange the matrix several other ways.

The best arrangement would probably be all the the postures down the side, all the postures across the top. That would be 100 combinations, definitely enough so that you could fill any blank spots, and you would have no misunderstandings concerning each technique.

Remember, you will find certain things don't work. Excellent. Sometimes it is more important to know what doesn't work than it is to know what does work.

Remember, a mistake is an opportunity to learn.

A PROGRESSION OF ART

Okay, we have Tai Chi resolved to basic moves, and we
have two man exercises, and you can line the basics up in a line,
and a Nine Square diagram, and we even have a matrix to give you
25 extra and intermediate techniques.

Here is a simple description of how techniques progress.
Interestingly, you can make a progression of techniques for each
art, but you will shortly find that you are mushing arts together.
The real progression of arts is from hard arts to soft arts. Here is
the progression:

A basic technique usually is one block and strike.

An intermediate technique could be two blocks and strikes.

An advanced technique could be one hard technique
followed by an (entry) soft (throwing) technique.

An expert technique would be one soft or flowing
technique. No need for a hard set up.

A master technique would be when you can stop somebody
before they strike, just by presence of mind.

So before we get into the throwing potentials here, let's
talk about advancing your form. What I am about to tell you can be
used as 'silk reeling' exercises. Soft motion that just moves
intention around without breaking.

THE USE OF ENERGY IN TAI CHI CHUAN

When you do Tai Chi your imagination is your main tool. You must do low stances (especially in the beginning), and start the tan (the energy generator) working. The energy needs to be directed by your imagination to become workable and fulfill Tai Chi.

For instance, one method I use is that of holding a large ball. If I am raising my hands I imagine the ball stuck to my palms. I feel the ball, and the suction of energy necessary to make this happen. I do this with my imagination.

If I am passing my hands, I am holding that ball. When doing Single Whip I am imagining that the ball shrunk, and is being lifted by one cupped hand, and drawn by the energy beam coming from my whip.

I do the form, or the sequence which might utilize that visualization, moving the ball about, shifting it back and forth, and so on and so on.

Separately, I often imagine a ball of energy pulsing up my legs as I put weight on them. This aids the generation of chi power in the tan tien, especially when I move the ball through the tan tien and down the other leg.

I imagine the tan tien pulsing and glowing, growing in glow and waning in glow, usually in accordance with my breathing and the particular move i am doing.

I keep my arms fixed and unbendable when turning my body, making my body one unit.

I imagine energy sloshing back and forth in my body, like water in a bathtub.

I move the hands to duplicate the motions happening in the tan tien. This is very useful, as the tan tien duplicates the hands.

There are many other methods of creating energy with your imagination. Imagining the muscles as musical strings and playing them.

Imagining your body in pieces, and moving like a solar system.

Imagining yourself fifty feet above the body.

Imagining yourself fifty feet up, and moving the body through the use of strings, or beams.

Focusing on shifting and dropping the weight. Breathing, feeling your breath swell through your body.

What is fun is to go through the nine square forms and implementing each of these imaginations, and whatever others you can come up with, one at a time.

Sometimes you will find one that really works. There is nothing wrong in doing just that one for a long time.

Sometimes you will find one that sets the hair on end. So move on.

BASIC APPLICATIONS
SOFT STYLE

Following are
suggestions for making the
applications of the basics
softer.

ROLL BACK
You could catch and break
the opponent's arm with roll
back, but you could also roll
it over, move his shoulder
up, search for pressure
points, and all manner of
wonderful things.

BRUSH KNEE
Instead of just low blocking
and paling the chest, you
can circle the low block, and
change the palm strike so as
to insert the arm next to the
neck. It is a little bit Chin Na,
and this technique is better

explained on the Matrix Kung Fu (Monkey Boxing) course, but it
really works to unbalance and turn an opponent on his head.

WHITE SNAKE
Instead of striking with the
fingers, you can turn the
striking hand over and grab
the elbow. This can result in
a wonderful sort of an
elbow throw or lock.

FAIR LADY
As in the Brush Knee, you
can insert the arm next to
the neck and turn the
opponent over.

POLE POSITION
The top block can turn into
any number of throws as
you are turning the
opponent's back to you. I
like the foot block, myself,
in this one. Merely fling the
foot and watch the
opponent twist for balance and fall down.

WARD OFF

Ward Off requires that one get close, but it is fun to 'ward' the body one way, and trip him over your knee. This is sometimes called 'splitting.'

WHITE CRANE

When your opponent kicks you simply do a white crane with low block, and continue the low block so as to grab his leg and turn him over.

SINGLE WHIP

In Single Whip you can grab, and pulse the energy into his chest. But remember that you have him spread out, and standing on two legs as in 2 dimensional. This makes it easy to twist him off balance.

There are many other soft applications that can be used, but I just wanted to give you an idea of some of the techniques I play with. The real bible of the grab arts is on the Matrix Kung Fu (Monkey Boxing).

The point here is to enable you to make a second matrix. One in which you use the first more to 'catch' your opponent, then use the second posture for a throw, or lock, or pulse of energy, or to manipulate on the axis, or use the limbs as levers, and so on and so on.

Remember, beginners use force, the next level uses force and flow (hard/ soft), and the third level uses only flow.

But the real thing to remember for the specific art of Tai Chi Chuan is described in this little saying I made up:

The attacker is the fist,
the Tai Chi practitioner is the 'glove.'

Fit your defense so that he lodges himself in you...'the glove'...then you may use gentle flow to do what you wish with him.

PUSH HANDS

Push hands is the 'freestyle' drill I use when teaching TCC.

Two partners stand at handshake distance with the same foot forward.

One partner pushes slowly, the other wards. They describe a horizontal circle between them, and when one partner has pushed far enough he becomes the warder and the other becomes the pusher.

The essence of the drill is to get out of the way without moving the feet. If you move the feet you lose.

This is a universe of force. People push and hit, and nobody takes the time to harmonize, to go with, to join the motion and guide it.

This is the essence of Push Hands, and of Tai Chi. To slip the punch without impact, to guide the attack to a point of unbalance, to empty the body so that nothing touches it and harmony is achieved within.

This is not to say that there are not strikes within Tai Chi, they are just not the main focus.

The main focus is to do nothing until nothing is left undone.

CONCLUSION OF THE TAI CHI

Let's consider the whole system of Tai Chi now.

First, you learn the ten basics.

Second, you practice them solo (in line), and you practice the simple applications with a partner.

Third, you get to the point where you treat the ten moves in one sequence.

Fourth, you perform the moves on the nine square, exploring silk reeling, and matrixing the moves on the nine square. This should give you 25 mini-forms, and the potentials for a lot more.

Fifth, you matrix the attacks, thus finding out anything you don't know, and becoming expert in applying the basics in a variety of situations, positions, set ups, and so on.

Sixth, you practice new matrixes with hard blocks, following by a second technique of soft motion.

Now, there are two other things you need to do.

One, you need to practice Push Hands, and any associated freestyle.

Two, you need to practice the large form, discovering new methods of motion, specialty techniques, generating energy in different ways, and, most of all, finding your way to more and more towards effortless throws.

At this point I want to tell you something: you have more understanding about Tai Chi and the martial arts than any person in history.

Seriously, nobody has ever applied logic to the martial arts, and certainly not as is done in the Matrixing method. So, enjoy, and remember one thing...

Do the Art until the Art does you.

MONKEY BOXING

For something to be true
the opposite must also be true

Al Case

A NOTE ABOUT MONKEY BOXING

I approached the martial arts with the idea of 'solving' them. Monkey Boxing is my answer, my solution.

As the years, and decades, passed, as I gathered more and more arts under my belt, I found certain things that didn't seem to fit into any other art.

I put these techniques, concepts, whatever, into a mental basket for later work.

Eventually I had enough material 'in the basket' that I realized that I had a separate art, a complete art, one that answered all my questions as to the art.

On the following pages I will show the essence of this art.

I do use forms, mostly classical, but changed so that almost every technique is a Slap/Grab. The forms I use are Unsu (a basic form I created and named after the most advanced form in Shotokan), Sanchin and Seisan. I teach one form on each belt of the system: White, Green and Brown.

The core of Monkey Boxing is the 'Slap/Grab.'

If a fly was buzzing in front of your face...you would slap it. This is the first move of the martial arts, a simple slap. Blocking comes 2 or even three moves later.

This is the crux of the martial arts. You would not swat a fly with a block, and truth, you would not likely even use a block in self defense. You would likely use a slap; the most efficient, intuitive motion a man has for self defense. It is the first thing a man will do in the event of incoming force or

threat: raise a hand and get that hand in between the incoming force and the face, or head, or whatever.

Everything else is fantasy. He will do this and I will do that. Fantasy.

So comes the question: why do we do Karate, or any other art? Why are we practicing these fantasies?

Because the fantasy arts enable us to learn things that a simple slap does not teach.

The fantasy of karate teaches how to sink the weight, how to align the body, how to breath properly, how to move the body in a coordinated manner.

Further, the discipline calms the mind, paves the way to cool, clear thought in the face of chaos.

A simple slap will not do this, even if the slapping method is arranged in method. At the least, it would take years and years to understand how such things as grounding the weight, coordinating the body, and so on, can be used with a slap.

So I usually teach Karate, or some other art first.

I teach it quick and fast, using the House methods, or the Butterfly forms, detailed earlier in this book, and I get the student to understand how to sink the weight into a punch, how to coordinate the whole body into a strike, and so on. Then I teach Monkey Boxing, the art of the slap.

The whole slap is actually a slap and a grab, or a 'Slap/ Grab.'

Using the Slap/Grab, and the following drills, will speed up strikes, speed up the body, and the ideas of grounding and breathing and so on come to the fore if the Karate lessons have been properly taught.

CIRCLE OF BLOCKS

Stand with one leg forward, the front hand in a low block with an open palm facing outward, the rear hand guarding the face.

Step back and to the side with the front foot. You can do a simple block with the other hand into the low block/guard face position, or you can circle the hands to the low block/guard face position.

The rear foot moves inward and forward to the front position. the hands move to, or circle to the low block/guard face position

This move is designed to move the practitioner off the line of attack.

CIRCLE OF BLOCKS W KICK

From the low block/face guard position circle the front hand back towards the body and over to slap the shin. Return immediately to the low block/face guard position

This basic is designed for the front hand to grab an incoming punch, to hold it while kicking under with the front foot.

You can do this as a two man drill, as a technique, and, when mastered, even in freestyle. The technique will work when the student has practiced it enough. If it doesn't work...practice more.

CIRCLE OF BLOCKS W PUNCH

From the low block/face guard position step/shift into a front stance (the rear heel may be up if the front foot is well connected to the ground) as you execute a punch with the rear hand. The front hand should palm slap the punching arm just below the elbow, on the fat of the forearm. Immediately return to the low block/face guard position

This will strengthen punches and coordination. When doing the technique do a slight sidestep and punch under the attacker's arm as you push it inward.

Do two man drills using these basics.

142

CIRCLE OF BLOCKS W KNEE

From the low block/face guard position circle the front hand inward and over to slap the knee just above the point. Return immediately to the low block/face guard position.

We don't normally kick with the rear leg because it is too easy for the opponent to see coming.

With a knee one is close enough that being seen is not a problem. It helps if your grip on the opponent is strong. Figure out a variation of this drill using the back knee.

Do two man drills using these basics.

CIRCLE OF BLOCKS W ELBOW

From the low block/face guard position step/shift into a front stance as you strike with the rear elbow. Circle the front hand outward and strike the elbow with the palm. Immediately return to the low block/face guard position. Figure out a variation of this drill using the front elbow.

After striking is is common, in Monkey Boxing, to apply a lock or throw.

Striking then locking is called 'shock and lock.'

Do two man drills using these drills.

ROLLING THE WALL

One thing we haven't discussed is striking with the front hand. The front hand presents a jab, which opens up the whole ball game, and must be developed for speed and follow ups.

Striking with the front hand is done with a simple roll of the hands, one of the hands being used to guard the face or body with a palm. One can strike right out of the low block/face guard position

Rolling the hands is an incredibly valuable technique because when the fight gets close, when the hands start to tangle, this rolling fist will break right through the logjam.

That said, I make sure the student practices a drill which I call 'rolling the wall.'

The two top figures to the right illustrate a simple half roll of the fist, the other hand protecting the face or body, depending.

The figure on the right is rolling the fist in a full circle. The guard hand should be moved (rolled) appropriately.

I make sure student matrix rolling the fists. so they can shift from the half roll with one hand to a complete roll to a 1 1/2 roll, as needed.

You can see, as you go through these drills, that one needs to analyze when and how much the hips should be twisted.

I also drill the techniques two man style, one attacking one student defending, back and forth in a line, or on any relevant footwork geometry.

The rolling fist creates a vertical circle, the slap grab creates a horizontal circle. This is in keeping with the theory of creating a globe of movement, and of energy, in front of oneself. A globe into which, should anybody attack, they will be mushed, smushed, swallowed up and spit out.

SLAP GRAB WITH TRIANGLE STEP

The slap grab is circling with the hands (opposing circles). One simply slaps, then brings the other hand underneath to grab. I train students to do this with a triangle step.

Relax the hands, feel pressure inside them, the pressure will translate to weight, and your hands will become very heavy when striking.

MATRIXING THE SLAP GRAB

There are two defenses for a basic incoming fist.

If the attacker punches with the right hand, and the punch is straight...slap his hand with the left hand (close) then grab with the right hand.

If the attacker punches with the right hand, and the punch is curved...slap his hand with the right hand (open) then grab with the left hand.

Do the technique on the other side.

Each of these techniques should be done with the following strikes.

Slap Grab and kick.
Slap Grab and punch.
Slap Grab and knee.
Slap Grab and elbow.

Thus, there are 8 simple techniques.

MONKEY BOXING GRAB ARTS

As the student progresses I give him more and more grab arts. These Grab Arts are simple locks and throws, a circling of the joint or attack weapon to a takedown. They must be simple if you want to make them work.

The Monkey Boxing locks and throws are detailed in the book/video course 'Matrix Kung Fu (Monkey Boxing).'

To make a technique work the student should first understand and use the 'Shock and Lock' concept.

As he progresses he may not need to shock and lock, but rather can just absorb the attack and throw it.

At all times the student should be analyzing and understanding the concept of not using force. He should anticipate the attack, merge with the attack, and use balancing (unbalancing) concepts.

The monkey boxing techniques are very logical.

They are based on the simple concept of circling the eight joints in either direction, with a few variations.

For a grab art to work it must be simple and direct.

A LIST OF KICKS

On the white belt level I drill the basic kicks.
front snap
side thrust
wheel kick
crescent kick

By the time the student has reached the green belt level I
introduce him to double kicks.
front/side
front/wheel
crescent/wheel

By the brown belt level I introduce him to more difficult
kicks such as:
spin (pop) rear kick
skip front snap kick (to the open side)
sliding wheel and chop (to the closed side).

I have the students kick air, kick bags, kick each other
(drills and techniques), and so on.

LOP SAU

Lop Sau means rolling fists. The one exercise I do which elevates all freestyle in my art, and elevates the student to high levels, is Lop Sau.

There are only six techniques in Lop Sau. Once a student has learned them his speed of freestyle becomes incredible. At this point I show how to insert the Monkey Boxing Grab Arts into the drill, slick tricks to watch out for, and so on.

The six pieces of Lop Sau are:

Front punch
Front hook
Back hook
Front kick
Changing sides
Changing with a kick

You will find that these six techniques, and their blocks, comprise virtually all the realistic striking arts.

1ST TECHNIQUE IN LOP SAU
ROLLING THE FIST

Partners face each other
at handshake distance, each with
the same leg forward.

Partner A strikes with a
front hand back fist to the face.
Partner B catches the
back fist with his rear hand palm
block.

When attacking move into
a front stance and turn the waist
along the plane of the feet.
When defending move into
a back stance with the hips square
to your opponent.

The back of the fist should
slap into the palm like a ball into a
glove.

The back fist simulates a
jab.

2ND TECHNIQUE IN LOP SAU
FRONT HAND HOOK PUNCH

Instead of striking with a back fist, partner A strikes with a front hand hook to the face.

Partner B executes a back hand high block.

Partner B punches to the mid-section with the front hand.

Partner A utilizes a 'dangling forearm' block.

Partner A rolls back into the circling fist of the first technique.

The drill is based on the constant circling of the fists. Any deviation is followed by a return to the first technique of the drill.

3RD TECHNIQUE IN LOP SAU
REAR HAND HOOK PUNCH

After the first technique is executed, Partner A doesn't move back, but rather executes a rear hand hook to the face.

Partner B executes a front hand high block.

Partner B punches to the mid-section with the rear hand.

Partner A executes a front hand 'dangling forearm' block.

Partner A continues the circle of the dangling forearm into the first technique of the drill.

4TH TECHNIQUE IN LOP SAU
SLAPPING THE FRONT KICK

Instead of striking with the initial back fist, Partner B executes a kick to the groin area.

Partner A slaps the ankle outward with the front hand.

Partner A circles the slap into the first technique of the drill.

You begin training this drill slowly, adding pieces slowly, and the speed of the blocks and strikes begins to increase.

In a very short time, maybe an hour or two, the partners are moving with blinding speed and never miss a block.

5TH TECHNIQUE IN LOP SAU
CHANGING SIDES

Instead of catching the back fist, partner A hooks the inside of partner B's arm and pulls. He should be stepping back with the front foot as he pulls, but only to the depth of his rear foot.

Partner A steps forward with the back foot and strikes with the new front hand.

If partner B has picked up on the change, and changed with the attack, he will catch the back fist with his palm.

If partner B doesn't change a big hole in his defense opens up and Partner A will touch Partner B on the face with his back fist to show it.

It will become apparent quickly that if either partner misses a block, is late, or deviates from the pattern, a hole in his defenses will result.

6TH TECHNIQUE IN LOP SAU
CHANGING WITH A KICK

As in the last technique Partner A executes a hooking pull with his front hand as he changes. Instead of striking with a backfist, however, he will execute a kick with his new front leg.

Partner B should change with partner A and slap the attacking foot on the inside ankle with his new front hand.

Partner B should return to the first technique of the drill.

THE PERFECT TECHNIQUE

The following list is a matrix. It was originally taken from a truth table, but it is simpler to put it in list form.

The Perfect Technique is defined as that technique which works no matter which side you apply it on, or to. Doesn't matter if the attacker strikes with the right or left hand, doesn't matter if you build your defense on the right or left side, the technique works.

There are actually a number of Perfect Techniques, but the last few moves of Seisan describe possibly the best of the Perfect Techniques.

The attack is a kick and a punch.

The defense is the sequence of moves at the end of the form called Seisan.

Block the kick with a low block.

Step forward and slap the punch with one hand and catch the punch with the other hand.

Move into an elbow strike followed by a splitting throw.

A splitting throw is one where the upper body goes one way and the lower body goes the other way. For instance, your right leg goes behind his legs moving his lower body to the left, you right arm goes in front of the neck and sweeps his body to the right.

That is the basic technique. Following is the list of attacks, and defenses, and you must do this list, in order, as quickly as you can.

You can do the list with one partner in the beginning, and strictly follow the list.

As you become. more proficient you can leave the list and have three or four partners so they can keep the attacks rolling in.

Right kick and a right punch.
  right low block right slap grab, elbow and takedown
  right low block left slap grab, elbow and takedown
  left low block right slap grab, elbow and takedown
  left low block left slap grab, elbow and takedown

Right kick and a left punch.
  right low block right slap grab, elbow and takedown
  right low block left slap grab, elbow and takedown
  left low block right slap grab, elbow and takedown
  left low block left slap grab, elbow and takedown

Left kick and a left punch.
  right low block right slap grab, elbow and takedown
  right low block left slap grab, elbow and takedown
  left low block right slap grab, elbow and takedown
  left low block left slap grab, elbow and takedown

Left kick and a right punch.
  right low block right slap grab, elbow and takedown
  right low block left slap grab, elbow and takedown
  left low block right slap grab, elbow and takedown
  left low block left slap grab, elbow and takedown

Thus, there are 16 self defenses, all derived from one technique.

The student whether doing the list or being the center of attacks, must figure out, on the spot and without error, the proper placement of the feet, the proper positioning of the body, correct distance, oddities concerning which side of the body is being handling, etc.

A variation of this technique is to have one kick and two punches. When one does this variation they should slap the first punch and grab the second punch.

By this time in a student's training he should have a certain degree of polish. However, I worry about them making the technique work first, then the polish.

THE CONCLUSION

There is no conclusion for the art never ends.
But my body will end.
The spirit will travel, but my work will remain.
Did I leave enough?
Can you follow along?
Can you step onto the Path of the True Martial Art?
Can you make your art whole through Matrixing?
Will you continue past your art and understand the whole martial arts?
And life?
The answer is within you.
Good skill and hard work will get you there.
My best wishes for your martial journey...

Al Case

MARTIAL ARTS VIDEO/BOOK COURSES

Matrix Karate

Matrix Kung Fu

Matrix Aikido

Master Instructor Course

Shaolin Butterfly

Butterfly Pa Kua Chang

Matrix Tai Chi Chuan

Five Army Tai Chi Chuan

Chiang Nan

Create Your Own Art

Blinding Steel (Matrixing Weapons)

Matrixing Kenjutsu

Matrixing: The Master Text

Pan Gai Noon

Kang Duk Won

Kwon Bup

Outlaw Karate

Temple Karate

Black Belt Course

Rolling Fists

Matrix Combat

You can find these courses and more at
MonsterMartialArts.com

MARTIAL ARTS BOOKS

Pan Gai Noon

Kang Duk Won

Kwon Bup

Outlaw Karate

Buddha Crane Karate

Matrix Karate: White Belt

Matrix Karate: Green Belt

Matrix Karate: Brown Belt

Matrix Karate: Black Belt

Matrix Karate: Master

How to Create Kenpo Karate: The Real History

How to Create Kenpo Karate: The Secret of Forms

How to Create Kenpo Karate: Creating a New Kenpo

Fixing MCMAP (part one)

Fixing MCMAP (part two)

Karate to Shaolin to Pa Kua Chang

Matrixing Tong Bei Internal Kung Fu

Bruce Lee vs Classical Martial Arts

Shaolin Butterfly

Butterfly Pa Kua Chang

Yogata (The Yoga Kata)

Binary Matrixing in the Martial Arts

Matrixing: The Master Text

Professional Martial Arts Instructor

The Science of Matrixing in the Martial Arts

Tiger and Butterfly: Martial Arts System

Al Case Martial Arts

How to Matrix the Martial Arts

Martial Arts 101: Fixing the Martial Arts

The Biggest Martial Arts Lesson of All (10 volumes)
Chiang Nan: How to Translate Karate into Tai Chi Chuan
Matrixing Chi Power
The Hardest Punch in the World
The Neutronic Motors of Pa Kua Chang
Monkey Boxing Forms
How to Matrix Kick Boxing
The Bodyguard Training Manual
How to Start Your Own Martial Arts School
3rd Level 6th Sense Sword fighting

You can find these books on Amazon

OTHER BOOKS

Neutronics: Prologue/Neutronics (volume one)
Neutronics: The Neutronic Viewpoint/The 24 Principles
(volume two)
Neutropia
The Simple Truth About Algebra
How to Make Your Own Secret Language
How to Teach How to Write

You can find these books on Amazon

NOVELS

The North Mansion
The Haunting of House
Machina (2 volumes)
Monkeyland
The Bomber's Story
The Lone Star Revolt
Yancy
Return to Monkeyland
Small in the Saddle
When the Cold Wind Blows
When the Black Dog Dies
Path of the Snake
Path of the Wizard
Path of the Dragon
Hero
Assassin
Avatar
Falling Skies
Pack
Twisted Gods
Lobo Love
Lobo University
Transformation of George Cogswell (short stories)
Light of the Insane Yogi's Eyeballs
Universal Glue (kids)
Return of the Dragon (kids)

You can find these books on Amazon

Made in the USA
Coppell, TX
04 June 2021